A Way Through

Healing From Loss
A Workbook

Kathryn F. Weymouth, Ph.D.

BALBOA
PRESS
A DIVISION OF HAY HOUSE

Balboa Press books may be ordered through booksellers or by contacting:

Balboa Press
A Division of Hay House
1663 Liberty Drive
Bloomington, IN 47403
www.balboapress.com
1 (877) 407-4847

Print information available on the last page.

ISBN: 978-1-5043-5910-8 (sc)
ISBN: 978-1-5043-5930-6 (e)

Balboa Press rev. date: 10/27/2016

Contents

Section II: Other Losses 29

Section III: Resources and Self-Help Techniques 39

INTRODUCTION

THIS WORKBOOK WAS ORIGINALLY WRITTEN to accompany ***What Obituaries Don't Tell You: Conversations About Life and Death*** (Weymouth, 2013), but as many people pointed out to me, there are other losses that may be even more difficult to get over than a death. The workbook has therefore been expanded to include other kinds of losses that you have experienced and want to work with and process. It is divided into three main sections:

Section I.   Loss Through Death
Section II   Other Losses
Section III   Resources and Self-Help Techniques

The workbook can be used with other books, programs, classes, groups, individual counseling, or as a stand-alone guide for individuals who want to process their own experiences of loss, grief, integration, and recovery. However, this is deep and challenging work that is most likely impossible to do alone. The important milestones in our lives are made more significant by inviting people to participate and be witnesses to the events. You may not want people to see your grief, you may have to search for the right people and the right group, but persevere. As much as I value teaching people self-help techniques, I am quite sure that trying to do all the grief and recovery work by yourself will not give you the healing that you want.

The work in the workbook will evoke many different memories and emotions. Since I know this to be true, why would I – or you - want to put a stick into this pot and stir it up? There are several reasons.

First, from each focus group that I did for *What Obituaries Don't Tell You: Conversations About Life and Death*, the number one reason that they gave was that a workbook was needed to go along with the book so that people who read the book have an opportunity and a guide for writing about and telling their own stories of loss and death. They pointed out that we seldom have an opportunity to talk in depth and at length about death in general, and even less so about specific deaths. The people whom I interviewed for the book were quite emphatic about the need to bring the topic of death, and all that surrounds it, into the public discussion.

Second, thinking and talking about death can actually enhance life and relationships, as counterintuitive as that may seem.

Third, preparing for your own death gives you a much greater degree of control over your final days should you end up as a patient in the medical system, where heroic but useless, painful, degrading, and expensive procedures will be done unless you have discussed what you do and do not want with your family, and you have signed documents that clearly lay out your wishes.

Fourth, having everything in place is a great gift to your family and loved ones and gives you peace of mind. Not only does it ease the burden on loved ones of making decisions when they are least emotionally capable of doing so, the grieving process is softened when they can look back and know that they did what you wanted them to do. As the funeral director who was interviewed for *What Obituaries Don't Tell You* said:

> *Don't waste your life fearing death, worrying about it. Get educated and pre-plan. What I've found is the more informed people are the better their experience. You don't have to worry about it anymore, the children don't have to worry about it, everyone can get on with their lives.*

> Gerard, funeral director

Fifth, if you are going to work with any aspect of dying, death, loss, and grief, you need to have done your own personal work around it. As a psychotherapist, one of my greatest criticisms is that many people in the helping professions have not done their personal work and healing. At the least they are not as effective as they could be in helping others, and at worst they can cause harm.

Sixth, unhealed loss, trauma, and grief affect a person every day of their lives, whether they are aware of it or not. Think about the emotional impact of a loss in your life. If you have not been able to express it, where does the energy of those feelings go? I can tell you where it goes; it gets locked into your system, into your mind and body. Whatever affects you affects those around you, and in ever-widening circles it has the potential to affect people you have never even met and probably never will.

The second section of the workbook addresses other losses in one's life. From the outside a loss may appear small or large, but only the person affected by that loss can quantify it.

The last chapter of the workbook is a list of resources and self-help techniques, but as I stated earlier, I encourage you to reach out to others and don't try to do it all on your own. Find a person whom you can trust with whom to share your feelings. See a therapist skilled in the areas of loss, trauma, grief, and recovery. Join a group.

When I ask people what helped them the most after a loss, many say that being with people who understand what they are going through without having to explain or put on a happy face was the most helpful. Others say having a self-care routine, or having something or someone else who depends upon them gave them a reason to keep going. Listen to yourself, ask yourself what might help you the most, and trust your inner guidance.

If, however, you discover that the only options presented by your inner self are to use addictive substances or to engage in dangerous behaviors to try to ease the pain, or to hastily jump into sexual relationships, it is doubly important for you to reach out for help as these are short term solutions which won't bring long-lasting relief. Do not feel ashamed or embarrassed or weak: everyone needs ways to deal with the difficult events and times in our lives, ways that help us achieve emotional equilibrium rather than creating more problems.

Before delving into the workbook I wish to repeat Marian's words from *What Obituaries Don't Tell You* in which she eloquently expresses the importance of doing one's grief work.

> *One of the things I realized when I was going through my own losses was that the only way out of it was through it. In the bottom of the pit, or the bottom of the well, you feel like you're going to drown, but you don't. I didn't drown, and in coming back up out of there one of the gifts that I've received is the sense of my own strength, and the sense that there is some way that extreme sorrow can flip to a certain kind of joy. It's hard to articulate, but it has to do with knowing the depth of feeling that's possible for a human being to experience, and grief and loss helps us to know that. It's that experience of depth of feeling, that you can feel as high as you can get low, the deeper your roots the higher your branches. Which is not to say that you feel happy, but the depth of feeling that you can be aware of, it expands your capacity for joy. Not just happy feelings, but joy, like deep engagement in the human experience. That's why I say you can go into that deep well and come back out with pearls.*

Marian Spadone
Educator, group leader

A Word to Readers, Instructors, Facilitators, and Students

There is something you must always remember. You are braver than you believe, stronger than you seem, and smarter than you think.

Winnie the Pooh

THE QUESTIONS IN THE WORKBOOK take you on a very personal journey about the process of dying, death, loss, integration, healing, and recovery. This is not an academic exercise in looking at death from a distance by studying cultural practices, but is a deeply personal process by looking at specific deaths and other losses, and how they have affected you, your family, your loved ones, your community, and in some cases the whole world.

The way that you decide to use this workbook will depend, of course, on why you are using it, whether it is for personal healing, a class you are taking or teaching, or in a group you are a member of or are facilitating. Even though the use of the material will be specific to your current purpose and focus, the material is timeless as different parts of it are more or less relevant at different times in one's life.

Some people object to the words healing and recovery, believing that you never heal or recover from a loss, and in some cases I would agree that full recovery and healing may not be possible. Certain losses are so tumultuous that they change the landscape of our lives forever, and those of future generations. Certain deaths are so traumatic that, as Pauline said in *What Obituaries Don't Tell You*, "The death of one's child is something we're going to have to deal with for the rest of our lives. It never gets better, it just gets different."

Deaths are not equal. We place deaths in different categories: timely, untimely, tragic, violent, unforeseen, deserved or undeserved, or those that seem so senseless that we can't help but ask, "What were they thinking?" The type of death, the relationship that we had with that person, our previous experiences with death, our beliefs, our thoughts and feelings about our own death, and our ability to put ourselves in the place of others whom we don't even know, are all factors in how we respond to and process a death.

If you are working with the section on death, the workbook starts by suggesting that you choose a story from *What Obituaries Don't Tell You*, or another book about stories of dying and death, to write about and then discuss, as it may be easier to read about someone else's experience to begin with. The material then moves into discussing one's own experience with a death by answering the questions in that section.

If you are working with the section on loss, one recognizes that losses are not equal, either. We place loss in different categories as well, from the trivial to the tragic. However, what one person may find trivial may be tragic to another, and vice versa. The lesson here is one of no judgment; neither judging oneself for how you feel, or judging others by thinking that they should be feeling and reacting in ways that they are not.

Throughout the course of working with the material in the workbook, strong emotions will arise so it is important for instructors and facilitators to provide a safe space for participants. This works best with a small group of people who build trust with each other by agreeing on certain ground rules such as whatever is shared in the room does not leave the room, respectful and attentive listening with no cross talk or unsolicited advice, and allowing people to remain silent if they choose.

Classroom instructors, group leaders, and therapists need to discuss support systems and networks for people using the workbook. People doing some of the work by themselves also need to have a support network in place. These may include a family member, a friend, the clergy, a doctor or nurse, a counselor, and/or a pet. If using the workbook in a middle school, high school, college, or university setting, it is a good idea to alert the nurse and school counselor so that these professionals can be resources if they are not, themselves, the class instructors.

Personal internal resources: Anchoring exercises

It is important that as people leave the classroom, group, or individual sessions, they have an internal resource that they can use any time they need to. Below are two suggested exercises and ways to end the session.

Exercise 1: Grounding strength and confidence

With eyes closed or open, have each person think of a time when they felt strong and confident, preferably a time when they did something they were not sure they were capable of doing but were successful anyway.

Using a scale of 0-10, with 1 meaning present but very low and 10 meaning very high, ask them to rate their level of confidence at the beginning of that event, then have them rate how they felt when they were successful at handling it.

Have them elevate the strength of those feelings as close to a level 10 as possible by adding statements to the memory and feelings, statements such as "I learned so much from this experience," or "my friends are so proud of me that I was able to handle this so well," or any other positive statements that a participant chooses in order to reinforce the feelings of being strong, confident, and successful.

When participants feel they have elevated their feelings as high as they can, have them anchor that feeling by clasping their hands together and holding for one minute while continuing to experience the feelings of strength, confidence, and success while repeating the positive statements.

After one minute have them take a deep breath, hold to the count of five, and then send the feeling(s) and the message(s) throughout their body on the exhale. Have them repeat the inhale, hold, exhale, and affirmations three times.

Exercise 2: Grounding peace and calmness

With eyes closed or open have each person think of a time when they felt peaceful, calm, and happy. Ask them to visualize the scene or to walk into it as if they were there. You may suggest that closing their eyes may make this easier to do.

Have them look around and note the people, objects, and colors in the scene. Ask them to become aware of the smells and aromas and breathe them in. If there are sounds, what are they? Allow those to register. If there is food, what does it taste like? Each of these – seeing, smelling, hearing, and tasting – will elicit its own feeling response, and the scene as a whole will create a feeling state within the person. Ask them to put words to the feeling state, some of which may be happy, relaxed, excited. If the scene as a whole does not elicit a positive state, suggest they go back to whatever was most clear and enjoyable to them in the scene and focus on that.

When the positive feeling is as close to 10 as the person can get on the rating scale of 0-10, have them anchor that feeling state by clasping their wrist and making one or more positive statements that reinforce that emotional state.

After one minute of holding the wrist and repeating the statement(s) have them take a deep breath, hold to the count of five, and on the exhale send the feeling(s) and message(s) throughout their body. Have them repeat the inhale, hold, exhale, and affirmations three times.

Ending the exercise: Grounding into the here and now

At the end of the exercise have participants do something that grounds them back into their bodies, like stretching their arms up to the ceiling while inhaling deeply, then bringing them slowly back to their sides while exhaling; walking in place for a minute or so while singing a song with a good rhythm such as "Row, row, row your boat," and bring concentration and laughter into it by making it into a round; have each person give themselves a big hug. There are many ways to ground, the object being to bring the participants back to present time, fully integrated back into their bodies, and able to carry on with their daily activities.

Section 1

Loss Through Death

To live in hearts we leave behind is not to die.

Thomas Campbell, "Hallowed Ground"

Choosing a Story:
Relating Through the Experiences of Others

A GOOD PLACE TO START PROCESSING a personal loss is to read other people's stories. The book, *What Obituaries Don't Tell You,* has stories of many causes of death told in the person's own words of what it is like to go through the death of a loved one. Included in the book are stories of deaths from heart attacks and heart disease, stroke, cancer, accident, suicide, murder, and unknown causes.

To begin with, choose a story that has meaning to you. After you choose the story, use the writing sheet below to guide you, first by writing out your answers and then using it as a basis for discussion. If you prefer, you can use a notebook or a journal in which to answer the questions.

As you read, memories and emotions will arise and you need to honor them. Pay attention to what your body is telling you. You may need to have something to drink, either hot or cold. You may need to warm up or cool down. You may need to stretch or yawn, be close to someone, or put a little distance between yourself and other people. If you notice that your mind is drifting, bring yourself back and identify, if you can, what caused you to lose focus and attention. Your body is a wealth of information for you, a sophisticated feedback mechanism, if you learn how to listen to it via physiological signals.

It is important to feel safe when sharing your experiences. Sharing needs to take place in an environment and with people who will respectfully listen to you without interruption and without giving unrequested advice. You must be able to offer the same safety and respect to others as they share their stories with you.

Continue to listen for and to honor your needs. As long as you are not doing anything that is self-destructive or harmful to others you are in the flow of the discovery and healing process.

1. Which story did you choose and why?

_____

_____

_____

2. What about it made the greatest impact on you?

_____

_____

_____

4. What did you learn from the story?

_____

_____

_____

5. Did the story change your perspective about anything, and if so, what and why?

_____

_____

_____

Deaths Are Not Equal

Weeping is not the same thing as crying. It takes your whole body to weep, and when it's over, you feel like you don't have any bones left to hold you up.

Sarah Ockler, *Twenty Boy Summer*

As has already been mentioned but bears repeating, we place deaths in different categories: timely, untimely, tragic, violent, unforeseen, even sometimes thinking that a person deserved to die, and those deaths when we say "what in the world were they thinking?" The type of death, the relationship that we had with that person, our previous experiences with death, and our ability to project and put ourselves in the place of others whom we don't know are all factors in how we respond to and process a death.

We also place deaths in categories, "cause of death." Death of an old person from natural causes, death by accident, death by violence, miscarriage, death of a child, death from disease or illness, death by suicide, cause undetermined; each of these impacts survivors in different ways.

How one dies makes a difference: the manner of death impacts the way we grieve, how long we grieve, and what kind of family and community support we receive. From reports of people who can communicate with the dead, it seems to matter not at all to them how they died, but it means a great deal to the living.

With the possible exception of deaths that could be termed "timely" because of old age when the person is ready to go, there is usually a roller coaster ride of emotions and questions that will never be fully and satisfactorily answered. Depending upon the cause of death, there will be questions such as "Did I do everything I could? Did I make the right decisions? How could this have happened? How can people be so careless or so cruel?" With a suicide the questions are "What did I miss? Should I have said something? Did I say or do something wrong? Could I have prevented it somehow? If only . . . . " These questions may circulate in your mind for weeks, months, years, along with the questions of "What do I do with this sorrow, loneliness, helplessness, guilt, and rage?" No matter which way you turn you can't find any answers that make sense or ease the pain. You are on a hero's journey, each day a little different than the one before and the one after, slowly but surely traversing the empty yet chaotic landscape of loss with its trials, tests, and challenges, but coming closer to some degree of peace with each step forward, each thing that you do to heal, although it may not seem like it.

My personal losses

In this section you move from reading about deaths that have no direct relationship to you to ones that do. There are three fundamental principles that underlie the exercises in this section:

1. We have all experienced death.
2. Not all of us have had the opportunity to talk about and process these deaths.
3. Some deaths have made very little impact on us, others have affected us deeply.

Making lists of those who have died

In the following section you will be making five lists of people who have died:

1. Family members
2. Friends
3. People you were loosely associated with
4. Public figures
5. Victims of mass murders

Deaths in my family

Name and relationship to me

_____

_____

_____

_____

Deaths among my friends

Name

_____

_____

_____

_____

Deaths in the community

People whom I did not personally know but attended the same school, organization, church, or lived in my neighborhood

Name and how I knew them

_____

_____

_____

_____

Deaths of people in the public eye

People such as politicians, actors, policemen, fire fighters, soldiers, religious or spiritual figures, and others whose deaths affected me.

Name and who they were

_____

_____

_____

_____

Victims of mass murders

Who they were and where and when it occurred

_____

_____

_____

_____

Going Deeper

Go back to the lists of family members, friends, deaths in the community, deaths of people in the public eye, and mass murders, and choose one person or one group to work with. If you are in a grief group or in individual counseling for the loss or losses you will most likely want to continue to work with this, although going back to the earliest death you can recall, or the one that affected your family the most, may give you new insights into your beliefs about life, death, loss, and grief.

If you are a student you might want to choose a death that is currently making the deepest emotional impact on you. If this death, or these deaths impacted other students in your classroom or program, this may give you an opportunity to work through the loss with several people who have many of the same questions and the same grief that you are dealing with.

An important note: This is the death or deaths that you will be processing throughout the remainder of this workbook, so you may want to consider several possibilities before deciding which one to focus on.

Working with the specifics

1. Write, then talk about who this person was to you, or these people, and why they were important in your life.

_____

_____

_____

2. For each question that is applicable, share as much as you know about their death:
* How and when they died.
* How old they were.
* How old you were at the time.
* How you found out about the death if you were not present.
* In your opinion whether it was an easy or hard death.

* What professionals were involved (e.g., police, Emergency Medical
  Technicians (EMTs), hospital staff, clergy, hospice, funeral director, others).
* The role of religious or spiritual beliefs, if any.
* The role of people in the church and/or other organizations to which the person belonged.

_____

_____

_____

_____

_____

3. Complete the Symptoms and Impact Chart below, then return to this section to write then talk about the emotional and physical impacts this death had on you at the time. (You will have an opportunity later to talk about how it is impacting you now.)

_____

_____

_____

_____

_____

_____

Symptoms and Impact Chart

Instructions for completion.
1. The emotions, states, or behaviors are listed in alphabetical order for the sake of convenience only, not in order of importance.
2. Mark each emotion, state, or behavior that you experienced at the time of the death, (or when you learned about it), and up to three months after the death.
3. Rate the intensity of the emotion, state, or behavior on a scale of 1-10, with 1 meaning that it had some but very little impact on you, increasing in intensity up the scale to 10.
4. You will be completing this chart twice, now and after you have completed all of the work in the workbook.

Example.	<u>8</u>	Anger
	<u>0</u>	Drugs
	<u>3</u>	Insomnia

0					5					10

none   extreme

<u>Rating</u>   <u>Emotion, state, or behavior</u>

Rating	Emotion, state, or behavior
_____	Anger
_____	Anxiety
_____	Can't stop crying
_____	Depression
_____	Despair
_____	Drop in productivity
_____	Fantasies of revenge
_____	Fatigue
_____	Fear
_____	Guilt
_____	Harmful behaviors
_____	alcohol
_____	cigarettes
_____	cutting
_____	drugs
_____	fighting
_____	over eating

_____   reckless behavior

_____   road rage

_____   sex

_____   starving yourself

_____ Headaches

_____ Helplessness

_____ Insomnia

_____ Lack of concentration

_____ Loss of religious faith

_____ Nightmares

_____ Numbness

_____ Physical pain with no clear cause

_____ Sadness

_____ Shame

_____ Sleeping too much

_____ Spaced out, not in your body

_____ Suicidal

_____ Troubled relationships

     _____   authority figures

     _____   personal (family, spouse, children, friends)

     _____   school

     _____   work

_____ Wanting to die

_____ Other

4. Now that you have looked at the difficult, painful, and challenging side of loss and grief, let's turn to the other side to see if there was anything positive, anything that might be seen as a benefit or gift for you from this death. For example, these may include liberation from constant care; closer relationships; appreciating life more; knowing what to say to others who are grieving; realizing your strong coping skills; signs from "the other side;" inheritance or life insurance money; property; seeing the importance of pre-planning; knowing what medical interventions you want or don't want; losing your fear of death; other benefits or gifts you experienced.

_____

_____

_____

5. How have the things that you listed helped you?

_____

_____

_____

_____

_____

_____

Interpersonal dynamics

Death does not occur in a vacuum; it affects everyone in the family and to a greater or lesser degree everyone in the same school, organization, community, and sometimes worldwide. Sometimes a death changes things for the better, e.g., when you are thankful the person is no longer suffering, the loss brings family members closer, or a humanitarian movement is started. Sometimes it changes things for the worse, e.g., when people blame each other; there is significant disruption to income, housing, and lifestyle; or it creates a pervasive sense of fear. Sometimes there is very little difference.

Focusing on the death or deaths you have chosen to work with, write about and then discuss the interpersonal effects it has had on the family or the communities named above. Include how it changed things for the better and for the worse.

1. In what ways have the interpersonal dynamics affected you, both past and present?

_____

_____

_____

_____

_____

_____

2. Do you and others have permission to talk about the death(s)? Elaborate on your answer.

_____ yes   _____ no

Questions About the Person who Died

IN ANY DEATH MULTIPLE PEOPLE and institutions are involved, personal beliefs and fears are revealed, relationships play a role, and for some, people who have already died communicate with the dying person. Any of these can make things easier or harder. You and others may or may not know about the beliefs, fears, relationships, and visitations, so answer questions 1-4 to the best of your ability. This section applies primarily to the death of someone you knew well, a family member or friend.

Beliefs and relationships

1. Did religious or spiritual beliefs play any part in the dying person's feelings about death? If so, explain and talk about how it impacted the death process.

_____

_____

_____

_____

2. Did the church or other organizations play any role in the dying person's last days and after the death? If so, explain and talk about what the church (clergy, church members), and members of other organizations did that you appreciated, or did not do that you wish they had done or should have done.

_____

_____

_____

_____

3. What impact did these actions or non-actions have on the person who was dying and on the family?

_____

_____

_____

_____

4. What were the unresolved, unhealed relationships at the time of death, and how did, or how are these getting played out?

_____

_____

_____

_____

Interactions with individuals, services, and institutions

With any death some or all of these will be involved. Mark each one that applies, and write and talk about how they were involved and what the experience was like. (There may be some repetition from question #2 above.)

1. Police or other law enforcement

_____

_____

2. Emergency medical technicians

_____

_____

3. Doctors

_____

_____

4. Nurses

_____

_____

5. Hospital

_____

_____

6. Assisted living

_____

_____

7. Nursing home

_____

_____

8. Hospice

_____

_____

9. Church or spiritual community

_____

_____

10. Organizations

_____

_____

11. Funeral home

_____

_____

12. Cemetery

_____

_____

13. Lawyers

_____

_____

14. Estate settlement, including banks, investment firms, real estate agents, IRS

_____

_____

15. Other

_____

_____

LOSS, GRIEF, INTEGRATION, AND RECOVERY

Death is not the opposite of life, but a part of it.

— Haruki Murakami, *Blind Willow, Sleeping Woman: 24 Stories*

GRIEVING AND RECOVERY IS AN uneven path. As much as I dislike the over-used phrase "life will never be the same," it is absolutely true when you experience a death. The configuration of your life, the life of the family, and the life of the community have changed. The grieving process may be brief, it may be lengthy, and it will probably be a back and forth, up and down experience.

The concept of recovery seems unlikely to many people who have experienced loss and they prefer the idea of integration. So let's explore what that means.

Integration is the acknowledgement that a loss has occurred – or any change, for that matter – it is affecting your life, and you are finding a way to adjust to the changes. This loss is now part of the tapestry of your life, and your perspective of it will change over time. When the loss first occurs it feels as if it is the entire tapestry, but with time you will be able to see it as a piece of the whole, how it has changed the threads of the tapestry, how it has changed the shape and the story of it. The loss section will always hold special meaning for you, may on occasion hold such power that everything else fades away, and then it too fades and you can see how it is once again a part of the whole.

With all that you have done in this workbook you have already been doing integration work, but there are a few more questions specific to the process.

Integrating the loss

1. Since the death, what has helped you the most with the grief and recovery?

_____

_____

2. What has helped you the least with the grief and recovery?

_____

_____

3. You have undoubtedly thought many times about how your life would be different if the death or deaths had not occurred. Write and talk about this.

_____

_____

_____

_____

_____

_____

_____

4. Are there characteristics and behaviors the person or the people had that you would like to make part of your life and if so, why?

_____

_____

_____

5. How are you expressing these in your life now, or plan to in the future?

_____

_____

_____

6. Are there characteristics and behaviors that you want to make sure are not part of your life, and if so, why not?

_____

_____

_____

7. Sometimes we don't give ourselves permission to state truthfully how we felt about the person or the people and their death because our cultural norm seems to be that we should feel devastated by every death, and that death somehow transforms the person into someone they were not. Is there anything that you want to express that you never have before?

_____

_____

_____

8. In your journey of loss, grief, integration, and recovery, what do you need the most right now?

_____

_____

_____

Complicated grief

The only time I would be concerned about the grieving process is when, after many months, a person simply cannot get back into the flow of life and find any meaning to his or her existence. This would indicate complicated grief. Some of the literature sets the timeframe at six months, but that may be too short a time depending upon the manner of death, the relationship with the deceased, and how severely it has disrupted your life. Sometimes grief lingers because of guilt, believing that you could have done more or made different decisions that would have led to a different outcome. Complicated grief can look like severe depression where the bereaved person cannot function, is not interested in life or living, and may feel as if they have been pulled into a black hole where there is no light and no relief. The aftermath of a traumatic death can result in Post Traumatic Stress Disorder (PTSD). If either of these are the case it is important to seek professional help.

I think that people who work in my field come to learn that grief is not bad, or it doesn't harm you. If it did, then we'd have the worst job in the world and nobody would want to do it for good reason, but it's actually not harmful. It can be harmful, but only if you really struggle against it, I think. So, if you can allow it to work on you then it does its work and something comes next.

Eric Fromme
Palliative Care Physician

Overview and Final Assessment

Y**OU HAVE BEEN ON QUITE** a journey of remembering, experiencing different emotions, processing, integrating, and learning. You have talked and written about a death or deaths that are very personal to you. As you have shared with others, you have heard about different kinds of deaths, personal and family dynamics, the grieving, integration, and recovery process, and much more. I commend you for thoroughly exploring an area of life that many do not want to acknowledge, let alone go deeply into.

1. Do you feel any different now about this loss than before? If so, how?

_____

_____

_____

2. Have you received any communications or signs from the person or people whose death you have been writing and talking about? If so, what were they, and if they helped you, how did they help?

_____

_____

_____

_____

3. What do you think the person or people whose death you have been processing would want you to be doing now?

_____

_____

4. Is there a way that you are, can, or want to honor the person or people whose death you have been processing?

_____

_____

5. Theoretically, what would you describe as a good death: what components would make it a good death?

_____

_____

_____

6. Theoretically, what would you describe as a bad death: what components were either missing or present that would make you describe it as a bad death?

_____

_____

_____

7. If someone you know is in their last days or weeks of life, is there anything in the readings, writing, and discussions that has helped you with their dying and death?

_____

_____

_____

8. If you are preparing to work in any way with the terminally ill, their families, or with services provided after a death; or if you are already a professional in the field, how have the readings, writing, and discussions helped you?

_____

_____

_____

_____

_____

9. What do you want to tell people about dying, death, grief, integration, and recovery?

_____

_____

_____

10. Is there anything else you want people to know?

_____

_____

_____

11. Overall, what impact has doing the exercises in this workbook had on you?

_____

_____

_____

12. Is there something that you would like to have seen addressed that was not?

_____

_____

_____

13. Final comments

_____

_____

_____

_____

_____

_____

_____

_____

_____

_____

_____

One Last Thing

A concept from the book *Even a Stone Can Be A Teacher: Learning from the Experiences of Everyday Life,* (Sheldon Kopp, 1985) has always stuck with me. He talks about events and emotions that we think we are over and done with, but at any time you can "turn a corner" and run right smack dab into them. One never knows when that will be or what event will trigger the emotions. What you will experience, though, is that each time it is different, maybe a little bit different, maybe a lot.

It is now time to go back to the Symptoms and Impact chart to see how your experience of the death or deaths you have been processing is different now than when it first happened. As you rate each one it will show you how far you have come in your healing, and what is yet needing more attention.

As you write and talk about your progress, see if you know what to do next to further your integration, healing, and recovery. You may already know, others may have suggestions, and you can consult the last section of this workbook in which there are many resources and self-help techniques.

Because of your commitment to doing this work, you are now a light in the Universe and simply by your presence you radiate healing to others who long for it. You bring the gift of understanding and hope to others who feel so alone with their pain.

Section II

Other Losses

At the temple there is a poem called "Loss" carved into the stone. It has three words, but the poet has scratched them out. You cannot read loss, only feel it.

Arthur Golden, *Memoirs of a Geisha*

Working with A loss

THE LOSSES EXPERIENCED IN LIFE are mini-deaths which require an acknowledgement of the loss; a recognition of what role that which was lost played in our lives; the emotional, mental, spiritual, and physical ramifications; and the need to process it just as one needs to process any death.

Below is a list of losses, and there may be some you need to add. These are listed in alphabetical order for the sake of convenience only and does not imply any order of importance. Mark the ones that you have experienced.

Loss of

_____ Belief

_____ Faith

_____ Health

_____ Home due to

    _____ divorce

    _____ foreclosure

    _____ natural disaster

    _____ other

_____ Homeland

_____ Identity theft

_____ Income

_____ Independence

_____ Job

_____ Love

_____ Meaning

_____ Possessions

_____ Relationship because of

    _____ divorce

    _____ a fight, disagreement, or getting dumped

    _____ a move

    _____ outgrew the relationship

_____ Religion

_____ Sense of safety
_____ Status
_____ Trust
_____ Other

1. Choose one thing from the list to write and talk about. Say what it is you lost, how it happened, why it was important to you, and how your life has changed because of it.

<u>What I lost</u>

_____

_____

_____

<u>How it happened</u>

_____

_____

_____

<u>Why it was important to me</u>

_____

_____

_____

<u>How my life has changed because of it</u>

_____

_____

_____

Symptoms and Impact Chart

Instructions for completion.
1. The emotions, states, or behaviors are listed in alphabetical order for the sake of convenience only, not in order of importance.
2. Mark each emotion, state, or behavior that you experienced at the time of the loss (or when you learned about it), and up to three months afterwards.
3. Rate the intensity of the emotion, state, or behavior on a scale of 1-10, with 1 meaning that it had some but very little impact on you, increasing in intensity up the scale to 10.
4. You will be completing this chart twice, now and after you have completed all of the work in the workbook.

Example.　<u>8</u>　　Anger

　　　　　　<u>0</u>　　Drugs

　　　　　　<u>3</u>　　Insomnia

0					5					10

none　　　　　　　　　　　　　　　　　　　　　　　　　　　　extreme

<u>Rating</u>　　　　　　<u>Emotion, state, or behavior</u>

_____　　　　Anger

_____　　　　Anxiety

_____　　　　Can't stop crying

_____　　　　Depression

_____　　　　Despair

_____　　　　Drop in productivity

_____　　　　Fantasies of revenge

_____　　　　Fear

_____　　　　Guilt

_____　　　　Harmful behaviors

　　_____　　　　　alcohol

　　_____　　　　　cigarettes

　　_____　　　　　cutting

　　_____　　　　　drugs

　　_____　　　　　fighting

　　_____　　　　　over eating

　　_____　　　　　reckless behavior

　　_____　　　　　road rage

_____   sex

_____   starving yourself

_____   Headaches

_____   Helplessness

_____   Insomnia

_____   Lack of concentration

_____   Loss of religious faith

_____   Nightmares

_____   Numbness

_____   Physical pain with no clear cause

_____   Sadness

_____   Shame

_____   Sleeping too much

_____   Spaced out, not in your body

_____   Suicidal

_____   Troubled relationships

_____   authority figures

_____   personal (family, spouse, children, friends)

_____   school

_____   work

_____   Wanting to die

_____   Other

Integrating the loss

1. There is a saying that when one door closes another one opens: sometimes it's true, sometimes it's not. If there was an opening or a gift from this loss, what was it and how did it change your life?

_____

_____

_____

_____

_____

2. What helped you the most in dealing with the loss?

_____

_____

3. What helped you the least in dealing with the loss?

_____

_____

4. You have undoubtedly thought many times about how your life would be different if this loss had not occurred. Write and talk about how you think it would be different.

_____

_____

_____

_____

_____

5. What do you need the most right now?

_____

_____

_____

6. What do you want to tell people about loss, grief, integration, and healing?

_____

_____

_____

_____

7. Is there anything else you want people to know?

_____

_____

_____

ONE LAST THING

A concept from the book *Even a Stone Can Be A Teacher: Learning from the Experiences of Everyday Life*, (Sheldon Kopp, 1985) has always stuck with me. He talks about events and emotions that we think we are over and done with, but at any time you can "turn a corner" and run right smack dab into them. One never knows when that will be or what event will trigger the emotions. What you will experience, though, is that each time it is different, maybe a little bit different, maybe a lot.

It is now time to go back to the Symptoms and Impact chart to see how your experience of the loss you have been processing is different now than when it first happened. As you rate each one it will show you how far you have come in your healing, and what is yet needing more attention.

As you write and talk about your progress see if you know what to do next to further your integration, healing, and recovery. You may already know, others may have suggestions, and you can consult the last section of this workbook in which there are many resources and self-help techniques.

Because of your commitment to doing this work, you are now a light in the Universe and simply by your presence you radiate healing to others who long for it. You bring the gift of understanding and hope to others who feel so alone with their pain.

SECTION III

Resources and Self-Help Techniques

Everyone goes through the grieving, integration, and recovery from loss at different rates and in different ways. Some of the suggestions below may seem a little frivolous in the face of deep grief, and they are in no way meant to minimize anything about your loss: they are meant to give you options that help in the moment and over time. We all need coping mechanisms, there is not a person alive who doesn't. Those who feel they don't have options for relief may seek ways that ultimately add to the sorrow and create new problems. It is not unusual for people to turn to addictive substances and behaviors as a way to ease the pain, or to jump into a new relationship too quickly, but the pain remains because these are unlikely to be healing choices over the long run.

The list of resources and techniques is in alphabetical order simply for the sake of convenience. They are not listed in order of importance or effectiveness; that is for you to discover. If you can't decide where to start, let that inner knowing part of you decide for you. Sit quietly while holding the workbook, focus your mind by clearly stating what you want to know (e.g., "what will help me the most right now?"), and when you feel ready open to a page in this section.

If there is more than one resource or self-help technique on the page, choose the one that seems most relevant to your question, write it down in your journal, ponder it, then write down your action steps. Later, once you have taken the action, write about that in your journal.

Using these resources and techniques is not limited to just loss and grief, they can be used whenever you are feeling like you could use some help and guidance with any type of issue you are facing, whether it be physical, mental, emotional, relational, or spiritual.

I know that our deceased loved ones wish they could ease our pain, so maybe these are ways that they can communicate with us through a gentle and unseen force that guides our hand in picking what will help the most right now.

A

Activism

Activism is a way to help you feel less helpless. There are many stories of how people have turned their losses into action to get laws changed or created; to form groups or movements to address a problem; to donate money, goods, and time to people in need. You may not feel called to do anything in this area, but even writing a letter to the editor, to your congressperson, or adding your name to a petition is a form of activism.

Altar

Create an altar to your loved one. Put objects on it that belonged to him or her, a photograph of them, and whatever else feels right. Make it beautiful and meaningful. How many times do people say they miss being able to have simple, ordinary, day-to-day conversations with the person who has died? You still can, and the altar provides a focal point for the connection.

Artwork

Art is a way to express feelings. You don't have to be an artist or have artistic ability in the limited ways that we typically think about art and artists. Art is a creative endeavor, and we are all creative. Painting, pottery, sculpting, these are some of the ways that we think about art, but what about making a collage from your

> The aim of art is to represent not the outward appearance of things, but their inward significance.
>
> Aristotle

photographs, images from magazines, and things that you find in nature? Decorate a cake, arrange a beautiful fruit platter, find the perfect color of paint for the room that never felt quite right. How about creating an altar that reminds you of your loved one with objects that represent that person's life and that speak to your heart? Do a collection of the person's favorite songs or poems or postcards and have a gathering to share them with family members and friends. There are so many different ways that you can express your feelings through a creative act; the only thing that matters is that it is meaningful to you.

Ask for what you want

This is self-explanatory but sometimes hard to do for people who are not used to asking for their needs and wants to be met, and often we don't know what we want. Almost always after a loss people will say, "Let me know if there is anything I can do to help," and they mean it, but they usually don't know what to do. Soon after a loss people are in overwhelm, and the simplest things, like making a telephone call, paying bills, buying groceries and fixing meals are just too much, so tell them what they can do to help you. Asking for help is a win-win situation: you get what you need, and they get to experience the gifts of doing something that is meaningful and makes a difference in your life.

B

Bach Flower Remedies

These are natural remedies that have been used for over 80 years to help people restore their emotional equilibrium and support healing. Information is available on the internet, with descriptions of each of the 38 remedies and a questionnaire to help you determine which ones would benefit you. Star of Bethlehem, for example, deals with shock, trauma, and loss. Rescue Remedy, one of the most widely available of the remedies in stores, is a blend of five remedies that help with emergencies, crises, and stressful situations of any kind.

www.**bachflower**.com

Bake something

What was the favorite baked good of your loved one? What is yours? How about baking those and inviting some friends and family over for a celebration of life. Creating a setting in which people can share their stories is healing. Often people don't know what to say about a loss, they don't know if they should refer to the deceased person once the funeral is over, so providing a setting in which people are invited to eat, talk, reminisce, laugh, and maybe cry is a great way to ease that awkwardness.

Bake something for someone else

The man who used to live next door to me was blind and the thing he said that he missed the most was being able to make pancakes. The hospice patient from the book *What Obituaries Don't Tell You* used to bake bread once a week and gave a fresh, warm loaf to the mailman. At the end of her life she requested that the hospice cook bake bread so that she could savor that wonderful aroma and enjoy a slice hot out of the oven. Who do you know who would love something that you made and delivered to them? Acts of kindness help fill your heart.

> I was the lucky one who got to take the bread to her with a big old wad of butter. She hadn't eaten for about three days and she cut a slice and slathered butter all over it. She said, 'Tell the cook I'm purring like a kitten,' and she went "Purr.'"
>
> Hospice nurse.

Break something, hit something

If you have anger or rage over a loss, including a death, you need to express it in ways that will not hurt you or anyone else. There are certain emotions that will eat us up inside and make our life miserable, as well as those around us, if we can't express these feelings in safe ways. Too often the admonition is to forgive, and that is beneficial in the long run, but you have to express your anger and rage first. Some people have gone to the thrift store and bought a set of cheap dishes to throw against a wall. Some have rolled up a towel and beaten a mattress while yelling out their anger and letting the tears flow. If you find, however, that over time these methods of releasing the emotions are not working, that your level of anger has not decreased and maybe even increased, seek professional help.

Breathe

So simple, but something we often forget to do while under stress. The breath helps regulate the sympathetic and parasympathetic branches of the nervous system which are supposed to override each other only briefly and under extraordinary conditions, then return to a more balanced state. Too much sympathetic activation and your system is over stimulated, in simple terms everything is too revved up; too much parasympathetic activation and you feel frozen, unable to function. A simple breathing exercise of a deep breath in through the nose to the count of five, hold for the count of five, exhale through the mouth to the count of five, then repeat this pattern two more times, will help bring you back to a calm state of being where you feel more capable of dealing with whatever is going on at the time.

Another breathing exercise is to put your attention on your heart or heart chakra, which is in the middle of your chest adjacent to your physical heart, and breath in a color, a sound, a picture, a word or phrase, and/or a feeling. There are many more breathing exercises available to learn about on the internet.

C

Call on a deceased loved one to help you

Whether you believe in life after death or not you can try this. One of my counseling clients had no one in her life whom she felt was trustworthy enough with whom to share what she was going through and what she needed, but she said that if there were somebody it would be her grandmother. She closed her eyes and made a mental and emotional connection with her and the change in my client was immediate: relaxed, hopeful, feeling loved and supported. So call on a person whom you loved and loved you, tell them what is happening in your life, and ask for the help that you need.

Ceremony and ritual

Ceremonies are important because they mark a rite of passage, a significant change in a person's life. A funeral is a ceremony and the commemoration of the life and death of a person. Taking flowers to the cemetery can be a ritual or a ceremony, depending upon what you do.

> The chaplain did a blessing where we were invited to bless the body part that we were drawn to do. She hadn't spoken for three days, but the ritual woke her up and she spoke to us.
>
> Friend/nurse/healer.

Prayers, doing life review, listening to special music, reading poetry, giving away possessions, healing, dancing, chanting, writing, a sharing circle - these can be part of ceremony or ritual in whatever ways you choose to use one or more as a way to acknowledge and facilitate a transition.

Counseling

Individual counseling can help you through the roughest times by helping you find the resources and techniques that will help you the most in dealing with loss and grief and re-engaging in life. Many people find grief groups helpful while others prefer to work with someone one-on-one, or combine group work with individual counseling and homework assignments.

People often wonder when they should seek counseling, and the short answer is when you feel stuck. If everything you have tried on your own is not easing the pain of loss; if after several months your emotional reactions are intensifying rather than abating; if your depression (and maybe fear) is so debilitating you can't leave the house, or you can't find anything you enjoy doing or any meaning to life; if you have slipped into addiction; if you fantasize about taking your own life to be with your loved one, then it is time to seek professional help.

Crochet, knit, weave

A new field of study into the benefits of handicrafts for dealing with emotional and physical issues is showing good results for depression, anxiety, Attention Deficit and Hyperactivity Disorder (ADHD), Post Traumatic Stress Disorder (PTSD), and physical conditions such as insomnia, arthritis and multiple sclerosis. The repetitive

> Today I am wondering: "How can I weave the strands of my life together to create something new?"
>
> The author.

motions of knitting, crocheting, and weaving create chemicals in the brain that help calm and soothe, with the added bonus that you can see moment by moment that you are creating something unique from your choices of pattern and yarn. Making something for yourself or a loved one is fun, and making blankets for babies, stuffed animals for children, and prayer shawls for people in hospice or nursing homes adds an extra level of pleasure to the project.

The book *Crochet Saved My Life* (Kathryn Vercillo, 2012) is the personal story of recovery as well as an overview of research on the benefits of crafts to one's wellbeing.

Cry

Cry as much as you need to and as long as you need to. Keeping a stiff upper lip, as the saying goes, is not going to help you heal. There are times when keeping it together will be necessary, and you will know when those are and will be able to manage it, but when it is time to cry, cry. Sometimes a person is afraid that if they start crying they will never be able to stop but that does not happen. Healing from loss happens more quickly when you express your emotions rather than burying them.

Cuddle

Cuddling is not just for babies and toddlers, grown-ups need it too. Caring physical touch is very healing. If you have no one to cuddle with but you have a pet, you already know that pets can be a source of comfort. Stuffed animals aren't just for children either; adults can benefit

> Physical touch activates the "feel good" chemical oxytocin and decreases the stress hormone cortisol.

from holding them, maybe telling them everything you are going through and how you are feeling. You may also consider volunteering at children's hospitals and animal shelters to give some cuddling, or volunteer to babysit so you can hold a baby or have play time with older children.

D

Deep dive into feelings

Tell yourself the truth about how you feel, go as deeply into the feelings as possible, wallow around in there for awhile. You will discover that paying this close of attention to, and honoring what these feelings need for expression, can be very therapeutic. If you are afraid that you will get stuck in some

> The deeper that sorrow carves into your being, the more joy you can contain.
>
> Kahlil Gibran.

deep, dark pit, set a timer for fifteen minutes, and when the time is up evaluate what has happened in that time and whether or not your feelings have shifted in any way.

You may be wondering why this is recommended when so much other advice is to "just get over it," "tell yourself that you're happy and you will be," and "what we focus on grows." There are two reasons why going deep is beneficial.

First, it is very important that you tell yourself the truth and express the feelings in non-destructive ways; and second, if you don't intentionally express the feelings they will express themselves anyway, possibly through physical illness, anxiety, depression, substance abuse, addictions, self-destructive behaviors, and/or behaviors that are harmful to others. From physics we know that energy does not cease to exist and manifests in some way. The energy of emotions has to go somewhere, it does not just evaporate, so expressing emotions in a way that leads to healing rather than to further misery is important. As you express you will find that the time comes when the feelings are defused. You won't forget, you will have times when you experience them again when an event or a memory triggers them, but they will most likely be less intense, of shorter duration, and you will be able to handle them. If you dive deep and express, and the feelings are still not defused, it is time to seek professional help.

Dreams

It is not uncommon for our loved ones to come to us in dreams; in fact it seems to be one of their favored methods for connecting and letting you know "I am still here." You may think it is merely your imagination or wishful thinking that has made someone appear, but a dream visitation looks and feels like no other dream: the images are clearer, the feelings are more intense, and unlike most dreams that are forgotten soon after waking, a visitation dream is one that you are unlikely to ever forget.

E

Emotional Freedom Technique (EFT)

This is a technique classified as energy healing, energy medicine, or energy psychotherapy. Using the knowledge of the body's electrical system, specifically meridians and meridian points, pioneers in the field of energy psychotherapy discovered that tapping on certain points on the body, and making statements about the situation or condition and how you wish to change it and heal, can shift the physical and emotional status quite rapidly. There are books available, YouTube videos, and downloads from the internet that help you learn the technique to self-administer, as well as practitioners of the method whom you may wish to work with. For an overview of EFT, also referred to as Tapping, and a tutorial on how to use it, go to founder Gary Craig's website, http://www.emofree.com/eft-tutorial/tapping-basics/how-to-do-eft.html Another good resource is Nick Ortner's work with tapping. www.**nickortner**.com

Energy healing

There are a number of healing techniques that fall under the category of energy healing, including Healing Touch™, Reiki, Therapeutic Touch, Touch for Health, Barbara Brennan School of Healing®, and Donna Eden's Energy Medicine. These techniques bring about deep relaxation, reduce depression and anxiety, improve sleep, and a

> In the last stages of cancer touching the person's body may cause pain, but Healing Touch can be done without touching.
>
> Nurse

feeling of connection to the divine, thereby helping people through the grieving process. Some of these techniques can be self-administered, but may be more effective, and more interventions are possible when done by a trained practitioner.

The underlying principles of these methods is that the body has an energy field within and surrounding it, that these energies and energy pathways can become disturbed resulting in imbalanced emotional states, illness, and impaired ability to regain homeostasis. With energy healing, these energy fields and pathways can be corrected so that the body can begin self-repair and healing. Energy healing can be done in the field around the body, or administered with light touch. Healing Touch™ is not massage therapy: massage therapy is an entirely different field of body work.

Information about these and other energy healing methods are available on the internet. Most have a list of practitioners in your area.

Essential oils

Certified pure grade essential oils are used for physical and emotional wellbeing. They can be dispersed throughout the air into a room, you can take a quick whiff from the bottle, they can be put in bathwater, applied to the skin directly, or mixed with a lotion. Since essential oils are highly concentrated and can cause skin irritation, be

> I used an essential oil for nausea and twenty minutes later I asked my patient, 'How's the nausea?' And he said, 'What nausea?'
>
> Hospice nurse.

careful how you use them. There are oils that help with issues commonly experienced after a loss, or while going through a difficult time as a patient, such as stress, depression, anxiety, agitation, and headaches. Oils for hope, peace, and serenity can help balance the emotions. To find the companies that produce high grade essential oils type "best essential oils," or "top-rated essential oils" into your search engine. From there you can research the companies and the oils that they offer.

Another recommendation is the American College of Healthcare Sciences™ (ACHS), where you can order oils, read blogs written by professionally trained and certified aromatherapists, and find research papers. https://www.achs.edu

Exercise

In asking people what helps them with their grief, many say that taking care of themselves helps with their physical and emotional wellbeing. The benefits of exercise are well documented in both of these areas: elevating your mood, lowering blood pressure, reducing stress, and aiding sleep are just a few of the ways that exercise helps you cope after a loss. There will be times when you feel immobilized, when exercising is the last thing you want to do, but instead of focusing on the negative, focus on the end result of how you will feel physically, mentally, and emotionally once you have done your exercise for the day. Consider getting an exercise partner to help keep you committed. Do something that you enjoy so that the process, as well as the outcome, provides you with pleasure.

Eye Movement Desensitization and Reprocessing Therapy (EMDR)

A therapeutic technique using eye movements and dialogue to treat trauma. This is not a self-help technique, it must be administered by a trained therapist. http://www.emdr.com

> After my father's death I just could not recover. I tried many types of therapy and EMDR was the one that helped the most.
>
> A bereaved son.

F

Flowers

Flowers and bouquets are beautiful to look at and lift your spirits. Color is vibration, and vibration affects you, so you can bring flowers into your life, or into others' lives, in whatever way you choose.

For a heartwarming video go to **randomactsofflowers**.org

Fragrance

Similar in their effects to essential oils, other fragrances can also help to elicit pleasurable feelings or ease distressing ones. The link between aromas and odors and brain chemistry is strong and has been well documented. Olfactory bulbs are part of the limbic system and directly connect to the areas of the brain that process emotion, memory and learning, and release hormones that affect appetite, the nervous system, body temperature, stress levels, and concentration. For some, smelling a loved one's favorite perfume, cologne, clothes, or aromas associated with a hobby can be soothing and make you feel less alone.

G

Games

Games, as in fun and games, anywhere from games that require deep concentration like chess to games that get you up and moving, like tag with the kids, to games that make you laugh. All of these are good ways to get your mind focused on something besides the sadness. Physical activity relieves depression, deep breathing relieves stress and anxiety, and laughter releases endorphins which promote an over-all sense of wellbeing.

Garden

Many people in recovery speak about the peace and healing they have found by working in the dirt. Whether it's a grouping of flower pots on the windowsill, a garden on your property, a community garden or an acreage, working with nature in this way helps bring harmony and balance into our lives and connects us to the natural cycles of nature.

My friends said, 'You need to get your hands in the earth, connect with the earth,' and it really has been healing.

A bereaved mother.

Gemstones

There is a wealth of information on the internet and in books about the healing properties of gemstones. You can carry a stone, wear a necklace, bracelet, or earrings made of a stone or a combination of stones, or have it in near proximity to you. For men, a pendant or cuff links are also possibilities.

Read the information about the gemstones that help with the issue you want to resolve, but also use your sense of knowing what stone or stones are best for you. Each gemstone has a unique chemical composition and therefore a unique energy pattern, just as you do, so you want to be able to intuit the one that is most supportive of you regardless of what the books say, then pay attention to how you feel when holding or wearing it. If you can, try it out in the store first so you don't spend money on something that doesn't work for you.

Get out

Get out in nature, go for a walk, go for a hike, go for a bicycle ride, go canoeing, go window shopping, go to a lecture, go to a concert, go to a play, go to a movie, go to an art gallery, go to the fabric store -- just get out and do something that nurtures your mind and spirit.

In her book *The Artist's Way*, (Julia Cameron, 1992) gives the assignment to do a weekly Artist Date to fill the well of one's creative spirit. But a date is not limited to just the goal of stimulating creativity; go on a date with yourself just because it's good for you.

Kathryn F. Weymouth, Ph.D.

Gratitude

Take a few minutes before you go to sleep every night to make a gratitude list, or in the morning as a way to start your day, or both. It's easy to do, just write down five to ten things that you are grateful for. It's not uncommon for people who have experienced loss to appreciate life and love more than they ever have before. You could be grateful for that; a deeper appreciation for life. Maybe the beautiful cloud formation that you saw, or the way your dog was so happy to see you, or the kindness that someone showed you. The items on the list don't have to be big and elaborate, they simply have to have meaning for you. Then read your list, lingering on the mental images and the feelings, really allowing them to penetrate your consciousness.

> There are earthly limits to love, but in his dying our love for each other became limitless. I just so believe in the power of love, which I am most grateful for.
>
> A widow.

Grief group

Some people get a great deal of benefit from attending a grief group where there are people going through losses like you are, where you can support each other in safe and appropriate ways, check to see what is normal, and have a chance to tell your story to people who want to hear it. To find a grief group check with hospice, hospitals, churches, therapists who list loss and grief work, and Meetup groups in your area.

Grounding

Grounding is a technique that helps keep someone in the present; it helps reorient a person to the here-and-now and to current reality in order to regain their mental focus from an often intensely disorienting emotional state. Techniques for grounding can be found on the following website. http://www.peirsac.org/peirsacui/er/educational_resources10.pdf

A common use for grounding is in the treatment of Post Traumatic Stress Disorder (PTSD), a state caused by witnessing traumatic events, the loss of life, and/or the fear for one's own safety. Symptoms of PTSD include, but are not limited to anxiety, feelings of overwhelm, disorientation, flashbacks, trouble sleeping, anger, and hypervigilance. First labeled as PTSD during the Viet Nam war, it can result from any trauma, not just war.

You can find instructions for grounding by typing into your search engine "emotional grounding," "spiritual grounding," "grounding for meditators," and other such word combinations. Support groups, counseling, and community involvement help in dealing with and resolving trauma: it is not recommended that you try to do it just on your own.

H

Healing Touch Program™

Listed under the section Energy healing above, this is the only energy healing method that is accredited by the National Commission for Certifying Agencies (NCCA). It is used by practitioners in private practice, in hospitals, clinics, and in hospice to ease both physical and emotional pain, accelerate healing, and ease the dying process. Individuals can learn simple techniques for self-care and to help family members, and for those interested in using it in a professional capacity the program offers a curriculum that leads to certification. www.**healingtouchprogram**.com

Another program that teaches Healing Touch is Healing Beyond Borders, http://www.healingbeyondborders.org

Homeopathic medicine

Homeopathy uses substances from nature to help the mind and body balance and heal. The Bach Flower Remedies discussed above are homeopathic remedies that a person can safely administer to themselves. Others, such as constitutional remedies and remedies for illnesses that are of a higher potency than are available for over-the-counter purchase need to be prescribed by a naturopathic or homeopathic physician. Some people respond better to homeopathic remedies than to pharmaceuticals, some better to pharmaceuticals, and some to a combination of treatments. If homeopathic remedies are prescribed and taken properly the incidence of negative side effects is very low.

> I cannot begin to tell you how much the Bach flower essence Rescue Remedy helped me with pain and emotional distress after my accident.
>
> Hospital patient.

Hugs

If you know someone who gives good hugs you are lucky, take advantage of it. As discussed earlier, physical touch is healing. If you don't have anybody to hug you, you can hug yourself. Try these different positions from the book *We Are All in Shock* (Stephanie Mines, 2003) and see what you like, holding each for at least 30 seconds. Each of the following positions is illustrated in the book.

Pay attention to your breathing. You want to be breathing a little more deeply than usual without straining. You may notice that at some of the holds your body takes a very deep, involuntary inhale. That is a good sign; it means that your body is responding to the energy and relaxing.

Hug your body by crossing your arms and putting your hands under your armpits. Hold.

Put one hand under the armpit and the other on the opposite shoulder. Hold. Switch sides and hold.

Put one hand under the armpit and the other on the upper arm. Hold. Switch sides and hold.

With arms crossed, place your hands on your shoulders and hold; then on your upper arms and hold; then one hand on the shoulder and the other on the upper arm. Hold. Switch and hold.

One more kind of hug to try -- hug a tree, put your face against the bark, sit with it supporting your back. People are sometimes labeled tree-huggers as a put-down, but if you have ever hugged a tree you know that the sensations of strength, stability, and life force are there for you to draw upon. Nature provides many opportunities for enjoyment and healing.

I

Invest
Invest your time and talent in something that benefits others. It may be paid, it may be volunteering, but somebody out there needs what you have to offer. If you aren't sure what you have to offer ask your friends; they will tell you because others often see us in ways that we cannot see ourselves.

J

Jewelry
One way to commemorate someone is to buy, or have a piece of jewelry made that has special significance to wear or to put on your altar. Some designers are now putting a portion of the cremation ashes into a piece of jewelry or into a piece of art instead of putting all of them into an urn or scattering them.

Join
Join with others in an activity or a project. Join a group that does something you have wanted to do but haven't for whatever reasons. Some feel a sense of liberation in being able to do something that their spouse was never interested in doing and now they have the freedom to do it.

Other people join or create a group to have others to share with who have gone through the same experiences that you have; you have common ground and don't need to explain or pretend. A book that is both life-affirming and funny is *Saturday Night Widows*, (Becky Aikman, 2013), **beckyaikman**.com/

> I remember one group where two women challenged each other to take driving lessons. It wasn't discounting the life before, but it was an invitation to become more who you are or want to become.
>
> Grief group leader.

<u>Journal</u>

Keep a journal. Writing about your experiences and feelings helps you process and heal. The act of writing, similar to talking, gets the contents out of your mind, giving you the opportunity to see events and feelings in a new way. An added benefit is that writing uses a different part of your brain than talking, so content may come out in writing that would not have otherwise.

A way to go even deeper into the discovery and healing process is to do the left hand, right hand writing technique. Starting with your dominant hand, the one that you use to write with most of the time even if you are ambidextrous, write a statement or ask a question, switch your pen or pencil to the other hand, close your eyes for a few moments, and when you start getting information write it out using your non-dominant hand. This will become a conversation, back and forth, asking with the dominant hand, answering with the non-dominant hand. Yes, the going may be slow, the writing awkward and messy, but you may be surprised at what you learn and how helpful it is to you in your process of healing.

K

<u>Keep on keeping on</u>

Sometimes it feels as if that is all that we can do, and it's okay.

<u>Kindness</u>

Somebody could use an act of kindness: it makes them feel appreciated, and it makes you feel good that you were able to help.

There is grace in the smallest act of kindness. It can help put pain and suffering behind us. Song lyrics by Cal Scott, The Trail Band.

<u>Knit</u>

See the section on crochet, knitting, and weaving.

L

<u>Life after death</u>

Certainly a controversial area, but one's beliefs can have a significant impact on the ease of dying, the medical decisions made by the patient and the family, and the reactions to a loved one's death. There are many books and stories about the survival of consciousness after death, by both medical professionals and people who report near death experiences. There is a great deal of information about this topic on the internet: books, articles, blogs, and research.

Live, laugh, love

Isn't this what those plaques in gift stores say? When you are dealing with a loss, these three things may be the last things in the world that you want to do, but let's consider a few possibilities.

> A merry heart doeth good like a medicine.
> Proverbs, 17:22. King James Bible.

Live Your deceased loved ones want you to live your life, and your family and friends want that for you, too. Your children may be lifesavers in many ways. If they are young, you need to keep going for them. If they are grown, you have people to talk to with whom you have shared many years and memories, and they will be able to talk about the person and experiences in ways that no one else can.

Laugh Hopefully, there will be many funny stories to share. Your loved one may even chat with you or remind you of something that will make you laugh. Some people seek out a sad movie when they know that a good cry will help them heal, and you can use humor when you know a good laugh will put you into a lighter emotional state. Find that funny movie, watch something on the internet, go to a comedy club, read a funny book, have lunch with a friend who has a great sense of humor. Your loved one wants this for you; he or she wants you to be happy.

Love Medical research shows that people who have something to care for, whether it's a person, animal, or plant, have better physical and mental health than people who are alone. Find something or someone to love.

You may feel that you are betraying your deceased loved one when you live, laugh, and love, but if they loved you, that is what they want for you. The message that they give via people who can communicate with them is that they wish we would not grieve so much. Sometimes they are close by, trying to ease the grief, but there is not much they can do so it is up to us to help ourselves. You will find that you can hold more than one emotional state at the same time, that you can be sad and lonely and still engage in life. You will also find that with time, engaging in life begins to incrementally lessen the sadness and loneliness.

If you find that after many months you still cannot find any pleasure in life, this is a sign of clinical depression and you need to see a therapist who works with loss, grief, and trauma. Short-term depression is normal and expected, long-term is a sign that you need help to heal.

M

Massage

Caring, therapeutic touch is relaxing and healing, physically and emotionally. Easing stress is one of the reasons that people go for massages. Numerous books and articles have been written about the benefits of massage, so

> Grief and loss can be highly stressful times, often filled with chaos and a sense of disconnection. Massage has the potential to provide safe pockets of quiet, calming respite.
> The Institute for Grief Massage Inc.

you can research it further as you wish. During a massage memories and emotions may arise, as our tissues hold our experiences in what is referred to as cellular memory, and if that is the case, and the memories are difficult to deal with, you will want to work with those in some way. Your massage therapist may be skilled in working with emotional content, and others will not be, so think about whom you will process this with should it occur.

Medications

It may be helpful to take a short course of medications to deal with depression and anxiety, but remember, grief is not a psychiatric illness and does not need long-term use of pharmaceuticals. Prevalent in our culture is the belief that everything can be fixed with a pill, and it just isn't so.

Meditation

There are so many different kinds of meditation that it is impossible to cover them here, but a link is provided to an informative article. You might like to learn more than one type, with the idea being that if you have several you will have the option of choosing the one that best fits your purpose at the time. http://liveanddare.com/

When it is difficult to calm the mind you might try walking meditation during which you tell yourself what you are experiencing. For example, "I am now lifting my right foot. I feel the grass beneath me as I put my foot down. I feel the sun on my face. I feel the air in my nostrils as I breathe in. My heart is happy." An advantage to walking meditations is that they engage the mind, the senses, and the emotions rather than trying to minimize them.

Another form of walking meditation is the labyrinth. The terms labyrinth and maze are sometimes used interchangeably but that is incorrect. A maze has dead ends, whereas a labyrinth has a path that leads you into the center and the walker retraces his or her steps to exit the labyrinth.

A common way to walk the labyrinth is to stand at the entrance, holding in mind what issue you would like guidance on or resolution to. Gently hold this in your mind as you slowly trace the path into the center, which is called the rosette. Stand or sit in the rosette and listen for guidance on the issue. When you feel ready, slowly retrace your steps to the exit. https://labyrinthsociety.org

Memories

Your memories, of course, will depend upon what kind of relationship you had with the deceased or with what you have lost. Sometimes it is hard to know if we should talk about our losses, but on the other hand, if they are not acknowledged it makes it seem as if the losses were not important. Sharing memories allows family members and friends to tell their stories, which frequently offers new information and new perspectives on the person or events. Stories passed down to the younger generation become part of the family history and inheritance.

Movement

See exercise. Get the blood flowing, the heart rate elevated, the mood improved. Dance, hula hoop, throw frisbees with the dog or the kids, swim, snowshoe, anything that appeals to you; there are so many possibilities.

Expressive dance allows the feelings of pain, loss, and fear of the unknown to emerge and hopefully be transformed.

Therapist.

Music

Stories have been told throughout the ages via music and can be a great healer: the tonal vibrations of music changes your emotional state. Music can evoke memories, which may make you cry and that's okay: sometimes we know we would feel better if we could cry and need a stimulus to evoke the tears. You may want to write some lyrics that express how you are feeling. It is not uncommon to receive messages from a loved one through music; turning on the radio at just the right moment, hearing a lyric in a movie score, someone sending you a link to a YouTube video, are all ways that we may get messages.

N

Near death experiences

Reading the literature about near death experiences, whether it be the reports of people who have crossed over to whatever the next state of being is and then returned to tell about it, or the research that has and is being done, can be comforting. The International Association for Near Death Experiences is a resource for both kinds of reports. www.iands.org/

Most people who have had a near death experience report feeling a depth of love and peace they had never felt before and lose their fear of death.

Nest

After a death, any kind of loss or trauma, or just feeling stressed and in overwhelm, you may need to retreat for awhile and just stay home where nothing is asked of you by the outside world. Snuggling up in the corner of the couch with a soft, warm comforter, maybe with headphones on listening to music, or reading a book, watching a movie, or taking a nap may be the most nurturing thing you can do for yourself.

O

Open a book at random or pull a card

Pose a question, concentrate on it until it is firmly in your mind, go to your bookshelf and select a book, open it at random, and read a line or two or a paragraph. How does what you have just read relate to your question? Does it provide any answers or insights? For fun, you can do this next time you are in a bookstore. Closely related to this would be to pull a card from a Tarot deck or one of the many other kinds of divination decks.

P

Pets

Pets seem attuned to their owner's emotional state and often respond by providing contact, cuddling, and comfort. For the human, they give you a living presence to care for and thus provides some focus and structure to your days. When asked the question, "What helped you the most through your grief" some people will say that it was their animals.

> I had this little bundle of pure joy. I'm not exaggerating when I say he saved my life.
> Rob Garofalo, Founder of Fred Says.

To find more information type in the words "animals as healers" and resources will come up: articles, recommended books, stories, and research.

Pray

This is self-explanatory; nothing else needs to be said about it.

Q

Quiet time

Time to be still, to be quiet, allows for healing and renewal. After a loss you may feel that you have to be busy all the time in order to keep your mind from dwelling on the loss and the empty place it has left in your life, but the busy-ness seems only to keep it at bay for awhile and does not provide healing.

Instead, go into the emptiness, feel it, explore it. Imagine that you are in a beautiful place all by yourself, feel the emptiness, the space around you, and relax into it and allow it to nurture you. You can imagine that you are in a huge cathedral, or sitting in a garden, or walking a golf course with no one else around. You can feel what it would be like to be a teeny-tiny version of yourself sitting inside a flower. The idea is to be quiet and welcome the spaciousness and peace of the emptiness rather than fighting it.

R

Read

Read for information or for entertainment, whatever you need in the moment. After a loss from death some people want to read everything they can find about dying, death, and the afterlife. There are scholarly articles, stories and books written by people who have had near-death experiences, and stories about signs and contacts from the other side.

When dealing with other losses you might find comfort and inspiration from biographies or autobiographies of people who have faced great challenges in their lives. And don't forget about humorous stories. Our loved ones want us to be happy.

Retreats

There are many different kinds of retreats, but no matter what the focus, a retreat takes you out of your ordinary, daily life into something new and different. Inherent in the concept of retreat, as compared to a workshop or a conference, is renewal of body, mind, and spirit, with time to be quiet and do inner work. To find a retreat for your purpose, type "grief and loss retreat" into your search engine and resources will come up.

S

Self-care

Self-care is inherent in all of the other suggestions. Take time to do it; do not feel as if you are weak or self-indulgent. The various types of self-care are your way back into life.

> I didn't realize until I got sick how little time I gave to nurturing myself.
>
> A patient.

Self-parenting, self-talk

If we were fortunate enough to have good parenting, what would your parents have said to you when you were sad or traumatized? You can be a good parent to yourself now.

Every age that we have ever been, up to and including this very moment, is still a part of us, so it's not just the us now that is impacted by a loss, it's us at all ages. It might be interesting to talk to your two-year-old self as if it was he or she that has suffered the loss. Explain it in terms that a child of that age would understand, give a hug, hold your young self on your lap, hug a teddy bear, whatever you can think of that would provide reassurance and comfort to your little self, and ask what he or she needs.

Pick one or two more ages to do this self-parenting with. Write about your conversation and actions in your journal. You will want to re-read this as time goes by.

Sew and quilt

Like other handicrafts, working on a project which requires focused attention shifts the mind to the external and away from inner turmoil. Watching something come into being that you are creating with your own hands provides a deep sense of satisfaction and pleasure, and maybe even more so if you are making something for someone who needs it or will love it. Some people will

The staff would pick two quilts from the supply donated by a quilting group and have the dying patient pick one. It was uncanny how one of the quilts would be a perfect symbolic representation of something deeply meaningful in their life.

Hospital chaplain.

make or commission a quilt made from a loved one's clothing, or a representation of things that they loved in life, organizations that they belonged to, or honors that they received.

Shock and trauma

Shock is a very big topic, too extensive to cover here, but shock needs to be treated. Shock to some degree among family and friends is always part of a death, even if that death is expected and welcomed. Does the dying person experience shock and trauma? That is a question that probably cannot be answered; it seems that some do and some don't. Many of the reports from people who have near death experiences say that dying is easy and they are not eager to return to the body. Whatever the case, the living have to adjust to the death. Traumatic deaths cause trauma among the living and result in more shock; if it was easy, peaceful, and timely, there will be less shock.

Death is not the only shock; loss of any kind can result in shock and affects people at all levels: physical, mental, emotional, and spiritual. The list of symptoms of shock is long, so suffice it to say here that you will know that you are in shock if you don't feel like yourself, you don't feel that you are fully in your body, it's hard to think, and everything feels "off." Sometimes you can return to homeostasis and equilibrium quickly, and at other times it will take longer, but if you commit to self-care you will not stay stuck.

Particularly helpful techniques to treat shock that you can use on your own, explanations of which are found in this Resources and Self-Help Techniques list, are art, Bach Flower Remedies, breathing exercises, Emotional Freedom Technique (EFT), essential oils, exercise and movement, hot or cold compresses anywhere on the body you feel is helpful, Tapas Acupressure Technique (TAT), and journaling.

However, trying to treat shock on one's own is not advisable. Being with a group of people who have experienced similar events to your own so that your story can be told and heard by people who understand, and working with a therapist who can guide and support you through the healing process, is probably essential for full recovery. Read more about shock and trauma when it manifests as Post Traumatic Stress Disorder (PTSD) under the above heading of Grounding.

Signs

Watch for signs. Receiving a sign or a message from a loved one is one of the most affirmative experiences a person can have. Messages and signs come in many different ways: songs, aromas, objects, synchronicities, audible messages, dreams, plants blooming out of season, something found that had been lost for a long time, an object moved from where it was last seen, feelings, feeling a presence – and all of these and more are signs that people have reported.

> My brother visited my sister, my husband, and me that night, the night he died, but we didn't know he was dead. Before this I would never have believed it was possible for a dead person to appear to you, would have said it was just wishful thinking on someone's part.
> A sibling.

Often we dismiss signs or do not recognize that we have received one, but some people never get a sign from a loved one no matter how much they want one. Does it mean that some do not send signs to the living? Does it mean that the living are not attuned to receiving, or having received, attribute it to wishful thinking? Nobody knows, but if you want one, remain open to the possibility.

You might also consider consulting a psychic or a medium. Some people have found great solace in hearing messages from their loved ones via this route.

Sleep

The most common sleep issue after loss is the inability to sleep or being afraid to go to sleep, but there is also the issue of wanting to sleep all the time. Suggestions for any of these sleep problems are Bach Flower Remedies, essential oils, guided imagery, and hypnotherapy.

Spiritual practice

A spiritual practice can be a firm foundation while you are going through loss, grief, integration, and recovery. Spiritual practices acknowledge that life holds great mysteries, that we are not entirely in control of our fate, and that there are unseen forces that we can call upon that will help sustain us.

T

Talk

Talk to someone about your loss, tell your truth about how you feel. Having someone who will listen to you without judgment and without giving advice is one of the greatest gifts you can receive, and if you are the listener, one of the greatest gifts that you can give. Talking about your experiences helps you process them. Events not spoken of tend to roll around in one's mind and gain momentum without the relief of speaking out loud and discharging some of the energy. It is not unusual to hear people express gratitude for being able to talk about their traumatic experiences.

There is, however, a psychological state called "shock talk." Shock talk is when someone talks non-stop, is not able to hear themselves and integrate the experience, and makes no progress in their recovery: it's as if a tape has been turned on and is in a continuous non-stop loop but with added side roads that are irrelevant to, and disconnected from, the issue under discussion. People who are in shock talk don't realize it, so help from a therapist may be essential to interrupting this pattern.

Another circumstance in which talk is not therapeutic is when people use their loss as a way to put the spotlight on themselves and will take practically any opportunity to talk about how the loss affected them, even twenty or more years after the fact. It is true that a death or other losses can have life-long impact, and being able to speak about it appropriately is healthy, but talking endlessly, particularly when it is about a death by making that death all about you is not healthy or therapeutic, it is narcissistic. Below are two ways to use talk as therapy.

Talk to the empty chair. Place two chairs facing each other, sit in one, and imagine that the person you want to talk to is sitting in the other chair – that person can be you or anyone involved with the loss. As you look at that person, tell him or her whatever you want to, ask any questions that you want to. When you are done, get up, sit in the empty chair, and from that vantage point speak to yourself in the chair that you just vacated. When you feel ready, switch to the other chair and continue this dialogue, switching where you are sitting, going back and forth until you feel complete with the conversation.

You may be surprised at how much information is available from the person in the empty chair as you move there and speak as if you were him or her. You don't have to force this, it happens quite naturally. Who do you want to put in the empty chair first? It could be yourself, the person whom you have lost, the person who caused the loss, an authority figure, a spiritual being, or anyone else. After your conversation is complete, write it down. You will want to review the information later.

Talk to the part in pain. Sit or lie quietly, focus on your body, find the part that is in the greatest pain, acknowledge the pain, ask if it is willing to communicate with you and if it is, ask what the worst part of the pain is, and ask what it needs. Pain can be expressed physically, emotionally, mentally, or spiritually, sometimes all at the same time. You may not know how to meet the need in that moment, but the answers give you direction.

> Dear Past, Thank you for all the lessons.
> Dear Future, I'm now ready.
>
> Anon.

Tapas Acupressure Technique (TAT)

This is a method that works with the energy systems of the body to clear stored memories and experiences that have resulted in emotional or physical issues. Whether the experience just happened or occurred many years ago, this technique can address issues no matter when they happened. For a free download which describes the technique and how to use it go to www.tatlife.com

Tapping

Thought Field Therapy (TFT) and Emotional Freedom Technique (EFT) are methods that use the energy systems of the body to clear emotional and physical issues. There are websites for each of the techniques. For a free download for TFT go to www.rogercallahan.com, and for a free download for EFT go to www.eftfree.net

Time

You know the saying, "Time heals all wounds," and to a certain extent it is true, but only if you use time to do your grief work. In physical healing the open wound closes up with proper care, but a scar may be left, that area may be a little more tender and sensitive than before the wound, and there will be the memory of the wound,

> The death of one's child is something we're going to have to deal with for the rest of our lives. It never gets better; it just gets different.
>
> A mother.

what happened to cause it and what was necessary to heal it. So it is true that our experience of loss changes over time, but time itself does not heal the wound.

Nobody knows where the saying originated. It could have been in ancient Greece in 300 BC when Menander wrote, "Time is the healer of all necessary evils," or John Ray in a 1678 book of English proverbs, "Time and thinking tame the strongest grief." But many losses are not "necessary evils," and "thinking" does not tame grief.

Time to grieve

Another use of time is dedicating a certain amount of time every day to grieving. This is particularly helpful for people who work a full-time job and for parents who have children, as jobs and family cannot be neglected. It also creates a certain kind of allowing and containment, freedom and structure: you give yourself the time but you also impose a time limit. Just as defining rules for children helps them feel more secure, defining these boundaries for yourself may have similar results.

Transformational Breathing

This is a variation of a breathing exercise that looks like the letter L if you could see the breath pattern.

Identify the emotion or feeling that you are experiencing that you don't want to be having. (For the purposes of this exercise the words emotion and feeling are interchangeable.) Name the emotion, then locate the place in your body where this feeling is the strongest.

Name the emotion that you want to have rather than the one that you are having.

Create a space about two feet above your head and place the name of the emotion in that space. Next, create something that represents that feeling, maybe a picture, music or nature sounds, a color, or a combination of these and place them in that space.

On the in breath, breathe in what is in the space above your head, breathing it in through the top of your head, down to where the feeling is that you don't want to have. As you are breathing in, tell yourself what you are breathing in. As you breath out, tell yourself what you are breathing out, and the space that opens up is being filled with what you have breathed in, what you want.

Continue this in and out pattern for several rounds. You will know you have succeeded in displacing the feeling that you don't want to have when you experience that what you are breathing in and what you are breathing out are the same thing.

An example. Let's say you are feeling loneliness, and you feel it most in your heart. You want to feel "not lonely," so you place that in the space about two feet above your head and create a picture and sounds that would represent that "not lonely" feeling for you. That might be feeling a part of a group of people having a good time, stroking your cat, someone opening their arms wide and embracing you – anything that you have experienced or can imagine that makes you feel not lonely.

Breathe in the picture and the feelings through the top of your head, breath them down into your heart, and let them settle in there. Then on the out-breath breath out the feeling of loneliness and say to yourself, "I am pushing out the loneliness." Do a few more rounds of this, spending at least three minutes, and check to see how you feel now. You may feel finished, or you may want to rephrase or re-image and do a few more rounds. This exercise almost always shifts you to a more positive emotional state quickly and easily.

Trust
Sometimes we have to surrender, knowing that we don't know what to do next but trusting that it will be revealed to us. Trust that the right people will appear, the right book, the right program, the right thought, the right guidance.

U

Upend
Get out of the rut of doing the same thing the same way; switch it up, upend routines. It doesn't have to be big changes, small changes will do just fine to create new neurological pathways. After a loss you are, in a sense, recreating yourself, and you can help that process by developing new patterns and new ways of doing things that belong just to you and are not linked to the past. Walk somewhere instead of drive, visit different churches, reverse your usual route through the grocery store: you can think of many ways, some of them really fun, to structure your life in a new way. And, of course, eat dessert first.

V

Voice your opinion
Maybe you have been in a relationship or in circumstances in which voicing your opinion and doing what you would really like to do has not been possible. A death, divorce, changing jobs, moving,

leaving a religion, each of these can be a liberating experience. What do you want to say? What do you want to do? If it does no harm to yourself or others, go for it!

Volunteer

There are so many people and organizations who need you. By virtue of the fact that you are you, that you have unique life experiences, education, training, personality traits, gifts, and skills, you have a role to play in the larger scheme of things.

Be alert to give service. What counts a great deal in life is what we do for others.

Anon.

W

Walk

Already covered in exercise, get out, and move: easy, costs nothing, and so beneficial it deserves its own listing.

Write

There are many ways that writing can help you. Write a letter to your deceased loved one. Write a letter to someone with whom you have unfinished business, either dead or alive. In a journal, write about your day, your feelings, your challenges. Write a letter to the editor and to your congressperson if there is an issue you feel strongly about. Use your words to communicate, to get involved, to be an agent of change.

Processing traumatic and stressful events by writing about them for 15-20 minutes for a few consecutive days helps bring physical and emotional relief. Repeat as needed.

If you would like to communicate with your deceased loved one, do the right hand/left hand writing exercise. With your dominant hand, write a statement or pose a question, sit quietly for a few moments to let the answer come, then with your non-dominant hand write out the response. Repeat, back and forth, until the dialog comes to an end, at least for this time. Keep what you have written; it will be interesting to look back on.

Write a letter to God

Write to God, or whatever ascended being or higher power that has meaning for you. Write the letter, say how you feel, ask questions, then write the response as if it is coming from the higher power you are addressing. You can use the dominant/non-dominant hand technique described in the Journal section or just sit quietly and listen for the answers and write them down.

X

X is blank

Allow your body, your intuition, or your desires to lead you into what to do next.

Y

Yes to life

Saying yes to life after loss has two parts. First, it is a way that you tell yourself the truth. Saying yes doesn't mean you like it, approve of it, or that it is easy: it means that you say yes, this happened, this is how I feel. Some will suggest that you sugar-coat a loss or do what is called a spiritual bypass. Platitudes such as "it was meant to be," or in the case of a death, "they're in a better place now," or "life never gives you more than you can handle," are examples of what others may say to you when they want you to do a spiritual bypass. Platitudes are frequently offered by people with the best of intentions; they don't want you to suffer and they don't know what to do to help you. Let that be their problem; don't do it to yourself. Tell yourself the truth because it is important that you do, and it will help your recovery.

The second part of saying yes is to find something to do that you can say yes to. Are you lonely, depressed, angry? Maybe reaching out to someone else who is lonely will help you both. Using one of the suggestions in this list of Resources and Self-Help Techniques may help lift the depression. Regarding anger, as long as your expression of anger does not hurt yourself or anyone else this is a very powerful, change-producing energy. There are many positive results that have come from people declaring that the status quo will no longer do, and by focusing the energy of anger into one of commitment great change is possible.

Yoga

Yoga has many physical, mental, and emotional benefits, offering a way to find flexibility, balance, and peace. Resources include on-line videos, books, and classes. Many people undergoing stress from whatever source report that yoga is of significant help in dealing with the situation.

Z

Zorba The Greek

Watch the 1964 movie starring Anthony Quinn, which has become a classic with its message of living life fully and with exuberance, while acknowledging and accepting that loss and death awaits us all. *Harry and Maude* (1971) may also be a great choice. Your friends may suggest a movie. Whatever the movie, the intent is to watch something that helps put us squarely back into living life fully by showing that life is multi-dimensional, embrace it, and as the plaques say, "Live, Love, Laugh."

Acknowledgements

The biggest share of thanks goes to the people who participated in the focus group to discuss the first draft of the workbook: Paul Laskonis, Joe Brookins, Vicki Chaloupka, and Dr. Pamela Paetzhold. These people were also participants in the larger focus groups for the book, *What Obituaries Don't Tell You: Conversations About Life and Death*, who urged me to do a follow-up workbook. Thank you for your encouragement and support.

The quotes in the Resources and Self-Help section come from people whose stories appear in *What Obituaries Don't Tell You*; people whom I have had conversations with about their own experiences of loss, integration, and recovery; internet resources and research findings; and information from my own experience as a psychotherapist and healer.

Special thanks goes to Cal Scott who has given permission to use lyrics from his song "The Smallest Act of Kindness." After attending a Christmas concert by the Trail Band I purchased the CD "Off the Wagon," and when I heard this song I knew it was perfect for the workbook. The song also appears on his solo CD, "Carved Wood Box."

Off the Wagon, by The Trail Band, trailband.com
Carved Wood Box, by Cal Scott, calscottmusic.com

Printed in the United States
By Bookmasters